New Immigration Secrets

How to Navigate the Laws of Finance, Business, and Real Estate to Build Your Future and Thrive in the New Era of The United States

By: Vijai Aanand

Dedication

I want to dedicate this book to all the hardworking, honest immigrants who come to the United States every year in search of the American dream. You are the fuel that sparks the fire in me, and I am honored to be with you along every step of your journey into success.

Acknowledgment

I want to thank my best friend and business partner, Amit for his support. I want to thank my father and my mother for giving me wisdom and creating a realm of extreme focus and self-awareness for every step that has prepared me in writing this book.

About the Author

Vijai Aanand was born in Tamil Nadu, India to a middle-class family, and he moved to the United States as an F-1 student to study and acquire a master's degree in Computer Science. He eventually fell in love with the systematic approach, the excellence, and the greatness of the United States of America. Today, Vijai is considered a true immigrant success story, building several successful multi-million dollar companies as a naturalized citizen.

Preface

This book is written specifically for immigrants in the technology industry. The technology industry has been an exciting field for many years in the United States. One of the number one factors that makes this a great nation is because of technology and innovation. Many of the greatest minds alive today want to be a part of that innovation.

This book is specifically for technology individuals. When they have this aspiration to be a part of something bigger than themselves, they need the guidance to be able to go there and bring their creativity to life in the quickest possible way.

The opportunities are boundless, limitless in the field of technology. Various nations currently are competing to get technology related talent within their own country.

The technology individuals could be software developers, software programmers, system analysts, quality assurance testers, prominent data cloud consultants, SAP project managers, or anything that is SAP related. There are many modules. The SAP individuals can be categorized into various positions such as project managers, product managers, and IT directors.

The technology industry has been very good to me personally. In fact, I would say the technology industry has been great. It's pretty fascinating when I look back on my career. Originally, I came from an electrical engineering background, but technology fascinates me because of the new developments that have happened and continue to happen in the few years that I've been in the industry. The innovation of technology has made an unmistakable impact on every country in the world in less than thirty years. That's unbelievable since this level of influence is unique.

To give you a simple example, there were certain things that we saw in cartoons several years ago like Inspector Gadget when the lady in that cartoon has a book which has a computer in it. At the time the cartoon was created, it was considered science fiction. Today, we have the iPad. Something that someone imagined decades ago has become a reality in this field of never-ending innovation. That "idea into innovation" mentality excites me along with other aspects of the industry.

This book wouldn't have been written or published

if it weren't for technology. I was introduced to my publisher through social media. That is unprecedented for our time. Technology is a significant factor in bridging relationships and creating opportunities.

This book is a guide for immigrants and individuals in the technology sector to find their place and contribute their greatest gifts.

Contents

Dedication...ii

Acknowledgment......................................iii

About the Author.....................................iii

Preface iv

Introduction..1

Chapter 1: Make Your Time Work for You 10

Chapter 2: Purify Your Mind and Body 21

Chapter 3: Increase Your Value 29

Chapter 4: Location Aligned With Destiny 34

Chapter 5: Financial Awareness 43

Chapter 6: Give First Mentality 59

Chapter 7: Overcome Self-Limiting Beliefs..........72

"I'm Opportunistic" 72

Cheating Mentality 75

"People Are Out to Get Me"...............................77

"No One Cares for Me" 81

"I Don't Need Others" 83

Postponing Talent 86

Irritation Towards Others 89

Chapter 8: Switch Off Your Clock 98

Summary...105

Page Left Blank Intentionally

Introduction

I have seen many immigrants being swayed away by external forces and making wrong decisions – simply because they don't know any better. To cut a long story short, there is a purpose in the life of an immigrant, but it takes everyone a long time to realize that. Throughout the process, they live unhappily.

Most Immigrants believe they have made a sacrifice because they left their country, they left their parents and loved ones for the sake of working in their adopted country. If more people understood that they have exchanged those things for something of greater value than the one that they left behind, they would be happier and more motivated to succeed in this new world of their choice.

If you are a non-immigrant on a work visa such as H1B or L-1, you might have been here for a while. Things, perhaps, have been the same way for you for some time now. You have hopped over a couple of hurdles. The further you go into this process, the more you realize its complexities.

Maybe you have the Perm labor certification approved, which is a first step towards the green card. You might have your I-140 (Immigration Petition for Alien Worker) approved. But this is a two-stage process, which takes almost a year to get approved entirely. Now once it's approved, you find out you have to continue to be employed with the employer until you can file the third step that is I-485, which is a ten-year wait in some cases.

You are stuck because you feel like that 10-year wait is too long, but at the same time, you are ready to wait it out. Maybe two, three, or four years go by. You might still be at the point where you say, "Okay. It's only another seven years. I'm doing great. I have some income. Things are going great. I have stability."

Because of the current environment, the US clients and also the new regulations support a "Buy American and Hire American" that is not favorable to immigrants. The clients are of the opinion that "Okay. We don't want to deal with this." You might be one of those people who feel this way. If you have citizenship or at least a Greencard, that is great. That's what people are looking for right now. The clients in the industry look for citizens or green card holders so that they can work on premises as staff and give them the solutions they seek. If the client hires a US citizen or a green card holder working for them, they have nothing else to worry about any other work authorization.

You know all this, but there is little that you can do to speed up your process. Here's another scenario that might happen to you, as it has happened to many others: suddenly, your application gets denied, or You might receive a paper approval (I-797) that says, "Okay. It's approved from, let's say, today to three years from now."

Then you get an opportunity for a project you are assigned, let's just say, in New Jersey. Then you get a project in North Carolina. At that point, before you make the move, your employer has to file an amendment, which means big changes, which also means location changes and everything else including salary changes. You have to move for that new assignment. It is only getting more complicated, and you just want things to happen already. At the same time, though, you know it will take its own sweet time before you get what you want in America.

It is true that things have only become tougher over time. In the olden days, you had more choice where the clients wanted the talent. In the past, if you were good enough just to have the technical skills, you could get a job anywhere in the US, and the employer could move you there. There is a staffing or a consulting agency, which is an employer, and then there is an end client.

The staffing agency could potentially move you to any other location that you wanted because you or they found a project in that area. Sometimes those areas do not want to have any immigrants working on their premises. Your choice as an immigrant has decreased a bit. Plus, the approval rating on the work visa is so uncertain. Visas have decreased. This started declining steadily over the years. Now there's a very low approval rating. Only 47 percent of the cases get approved

You, as an immigrant, have a fear now. You will possibly think, "Let me work at this low rate because I have the security. I'll work at this lower rate. I just live here even if I don't like that job. Then if it's approved, I'm good. This is one part of you that tells you to just be as you are and somehow pull it along as much as possible, and then let's see what happens. I really don't think I'm committed enough to wait the ten years. I don't believe that they want me anymore because of the Administration, or because of my talent." Do you see how your citizenship – its lack, I mean – limits your options and restricts your success?

Another thing that you might do is tell yourself a lie. This is when you wonder that maybe this is not for you. It is very easy for you to think such things as, "I can work anywhere in my home county. Why would I want to suffer here for every time I move whether the petition is going to be approved?" This is too much pressure for you. In the olden days, if you had one approval by filing just an LCA, which is just a few minutes approval, you'd be allowed to move to a different location, which was much easier. Now the United States Citizenship and Immigration Services (USCIS) want a new petition filed, which is more expensive for the employer, and there is more anxiety for you.

Maybe you feel, "There's no security. I got this I-140 approved, which is the second stage. I waited all these years to get that thing approved. I see other people doing better, but I really don't know what they are doing." As an immigrant, you might see other people making more money at some other technology. You might also have to face pressure from home that if you can't support the whole thing, it might be better for you to come back. In all of this, you have to grapple with the fear that if you go back to your home country, you can never come back to America.

If these are the thoughts that are running through your head as an immigrant to the United States of America, this is the book for you. I have written it to provide you with a blueprint on how to mitigate the situation of immigration. You might not believe it, but there is nothing in your story of applications, amendments, and rejections that has not happened before.

I remember the day that I landed in Newark Airport. It's a funny story. I recall walking to the immigration counter after I got off the airline. My dad warned me, "There are many criminals out in the US and then the outside world. I need you to be extremely careful." I was extremely cautious. As I was walking along, I just checked my pocket. I couldn't find my passport. Then I looked at the person right behind me in the eye. This was the thief who had taken my passport.

As I looked at him, he looked back at me with uneasiness. I said to myself, "Okay. I might have to wait here because if I go, my turn comes too quickly. I don't have the passport. They might detain me and send me back to India." I started waiting there. Then I said, "Wait a minute. Let me even check my entire bag." I started taking out one by one everything from my bag and found my passport in that. Then I went to the official person, gave them my passport at the immigration counter.

I was asked, "Why are you going to the United States?" I replied, "To study." Then I entered the country. Outside, there was a small store, a coffee store. I look at my wallet. I think I had five bucks or something at that time because I had exchanged the money, the Indian rupees I had, to US dollars. I only had 100 bucks in all; my dad had told me he'd wire more money later. Then, a bad coffee, i.e. black coffee and many scares later, I started out my life in this country.

Today I have two multimillion-dollar businesses. I have 150 plus employees. That's where I'm at presently, and I started out at the very bottom. Through this book, I am going to tell you that you can do the same. I had tough times. But I'm glad that I stayed and followed through on my dream. From the bad coffee and the five dollars to multimillion-dollar companies, it has been quite a ride. This is my personal success story which I have written to show you that yes, you can do it, too.

This is for all the immigrants who want to make America their country.

You are skilled and talented. You are kind. You resonate the American values because you are as adaptable as water. You now only have to go towards your destination. This is the essence of this book. I want to share my story and help others with their citizenship and the green card processes in this country. The green card takes ten years, and citizenship is just five years from then. That will be your turning point, just as it was mine. I hope my story will keep you moving forward. The time is now: decide that you will be somebody who provides value and you will become that person.

Start by asking yourself if you are in this for the long term. Once you make up your mind like I did, I can assure you that you will be successful and happy. Your time here has only begun. You will thrive in this land of opportunities because you are full of potential. Believe that you are born to be extraordinary. Believe you can do great things. This is the country that you have chosen to make your home – and let me tell you that this country will choose you too provided you take action on the principles you will learn in this book.

Bring all your strengths to the table. This is the only place in the world where you can move mountains like you are destined to. You will hit big because you have got what it takes to make it. It is important to follow the sequence in this book as things done in sequence will only give the best result. An example would be if you need to drop your kid to school, give him a bath and cloth him or her, the right sequence would be to give him/her a bath, cloth them and then drop them to school. If you do it out of sequence, it is a disaster. Agreed? Now, let's proceed with commitment and courage and learn the keys towards your financial, physical and mental well-being.

Chapter 1: Make Your Time Work for You

People have time on their hands and then what do they do? Do they do great things, productive things, or things that would take them closer to their goal? Or is it that they just live through their life without making their time work for them? I know of many people who watch their hours turn into days and days into weeks into months into years... When they look back, they realize years have passed. That's what happened to my dad. Let me share that story.

When I was a little boy, my father used to work as a sales engineer in Umm Al Quwain Asbestos Company. I, my mom and my sister used to live with him in Dubai. He lived in the United Arab Emirates for more than 25 years. That's how much time he spent there. I didn't live with him that long myself. I just went there for a few years. However, my father is a different story entirely. During the entire 25years of his employment, he just grew linearly in the company. He was one of the longest-serving employees for that entire organization.

Many times, he used to say things to me such as, "When I came to the United Arab Emirates, I didn't know the car was a great investment. I just found out that out. I always thought a car was very expensive. I used to take the office bus to go to work." It was only several years later, maybe five or ten years after he first went there, that he bought his first car. It was a Honda Civic.

That was also a green car, and he got it because it was not too expensive. You know why he had never bought a car before? It was because he was so very fearful of investing in a car. He thought that a car would not return his investment. He believed cars depreciate. My father thought, "Let me not spend too much and see how it works."

In the end, he invested $2000 (dirhams 6000) and got his car. It made him so happy. I remember he was so happy when he got the car. A year after he got the car, he said, "I didn't know that this particular amount that I spent on the car would give me a lot of freedom to be able to travel to different Emirates." Each Emirate is comparable to a state in the US. When he got the car, he had the mobility to travel to all the states. He met a lot of interesting people which he never would have if he hadn't bought his car. He said this was the missing link nobody gave him. The benefits of this investment went further than financial returns. My father said, "If I'd had this link I would've been able to purchase this car way earlier on. This would've opened more doors for various businesses. Because of my car I met various contacts that I could've met earlier on in life. This would have given me better progress."

This is just one of the things he said to me. He actually related so many incidents to me. For example, he had an opportunity to meet the right-hand of the Sheikh on one occasion. He said, "I could've met this person a long time ago, but I didn't know that my secretary was actually one of their contacts because we never talked about it. If I had just known this missing link, I would've been able to go and meet this Sheikh directly. I would probably do something different than what I've been doing."

As I heard my father make this connection over and over again, I started thinking that the solution lies right in front of our eyes. Our job is to look at it, believe that it is there and find it. And it's not just good enough to merely find it. You should also take necessary action.

In Napoleon Hill's Think and Grow Rich, he says that in

life, you are given an envelope which has two envelopes. One has the key to success, the other one has the price to pay for failure. Essentially, those are the two envelopes that are right in front of you. All you have do is choose the envelope for success, and the universe will open up for you. The universe itself will give you success.

What I got from that was the key to success, the same key that we look for in books and in motivational speeches and whatnot is actually provided to us. It is right in front of you; you have it as soon as you are born. However, in order to open the door to success, you need to have the energy to pick up the key, put it in the door, and then open it.

You know what's in your hands? The power to build the energy in order to do all of the acts. That is what's in your hands! How do you build energy? It is, again, a very small thing. To build energy you have to feed yourself with the necessary ingredients that give you energy. Then you have to take the action of picking up the key and then opening the door of success. All these acts of feeding yourself, building your energy, do you know what they are called? They are called acts of investing in yourself.

Let's go back to the example of my dad. If he had

invested in that car earlier on, he would have had a better advantage. Most people want the missing link without investing in themselves. They want those things for free. But in reality, you have to pay the price, either in terms of money or in terms of time. Now money can be unlimited. You can make an unlimited amount of money, but do you know the deal about time? There is only so much time in a day and in your life. You can't make time like you can make money.

What type of trade do you want to make? Do you want to invest money so that you can buy time? Or do you want to go faster than time? Or do you want to just wait for a free time when the universe would open its key for you? Either way, you are investing in that. Either your time or your money – you have to make the investment. My approach to this is quite straightforward. Investing your money in the things that will pay off for you later. If you do that, those small sums of money, if you invest them wisely, will take you a long way. The universe will help you because it is its job to help. The universe, believe it, is created to help you succeed. That's my true belief.

Now, I might have read close to 500 books so far. Reading 500 books, of course, did not happen overnight.

When I was in college, I couldn't even afford those books. There was this one book called Rich Dad and Poor Dad that I wanted to read but could not afford. Around the same time, I heard from a friend that Charles Schwab liked Barnes & Nobles in his early days, and he went there to read books. He used to go there and just read some random books. I'm not sure if that was a true story or not, but I took it to heart.

In those days, I made $6 an hour working as a desk attendant at the New Jersey Institute of Technology. After listening to that story, what I decided was, "Okay, spending $6 to buy a book is a lot of money, and I cannot afford to buy the book. What I will do is spend an hour of investment in the book." Another fact is that I love New York. What I decided was that I'm going to go to New York City almost every weekend. I was going to use $1 for the path to go and $1 to come back. If I ever needed a sandwich, I'd just pay six bucks. The total trip took less than 10 bucks, and with that amount, I could go to New York City and feel alive. That was, according to me, the most happening place on Earth.

I used to go to New York and move around. I often used to end up on different streets. One day, I ended up in

Barnes and Nobles. That's where I started to read the books I wanted to read. As I read, I also jotted down all the points that I needed to work on. This was the process for me to gather the knowledge that I needed. Another idea would be to go to the local library or get audible from a digital library which is some of the options available these days which were not available 10 to 15 years ago.

That's the method I recommend because there's not a lot of investment in the beginning unless you find some book is really awesome, where you feel you have to own that book. Personally, I feel that owning books because it can always help you refer back to it. In the Indian culture, we were taught that basically, the goddess of education (Saraswathi) does not come to you if you do not pay the price for that. In other words, if you want to get free education from YouTube or something, it will be incomplete, and you will not gain the full benefit from it.

That's the method I recommend - learn through books. Read books, absorb their knowledge and apply what you learn in your life. In the Indian culture, we were taught that the Goddess of education does not come to you if you do not pay the price for that. I applied that law and purchased the book Rich Dad, Poor Dad. This was one of the first few books I purchased other than my college books. This book explained how a rich dad thinks and how a poor dad thinks. It was through reading this book that I found out my dad was always the poor dad in that sense.

That's when I made the commitment that I am going to take the rich dad from this book. My dad didn't give me the rich dad advice, but this book gave it to me. I knew if I wanted to be rich I had to have a rich dad advising me. That's how I started reading and applying the information.

I made an investment after I read this book. Let me share that story with you.

I was really thrilled with the idea presented in this book. I mean both me and my business partner; he was and still is my friend. He got a job in Florida, and he had to move away. The following day he said to me, "Hey I have to go and take this job now that I'm moving away to Florida." At that time, he was only my best friend. We didn't have a business together. We just had a couple of drinks together and expressed how completely unhappy we were that we had to part ways. And then I turned to him and said, "Okay, wait a minute. I want to quit whatever I'm doing here searching for jobs on the internet, and I want to join you."

He was thrilled with the idea! He said, "You are going to join me and leave from here to Florida?"

I said, "Yeah, yeah, let's just do it. I'm going to figure this out later, but I'm going to move now. I'm not going to let this thing go because either way, I'm still looking for a job." I moved to Florida. My friend said to me, "Let's implement the stuff. We've been reading too much. Let's do something. You read about real estate, you read about all these things, and we're not doing anything, and I'm fed up with the whole thing." I said, "Okay, definitely, I'm willing to work with you on that."

We decided we'd buy a house or a real estate property. It was a tough thing, but my friend said he was confident I could do it. At that point, we started looking out for properties. But first I decided we needed to have a lawyer. I got the lawyer, who cost us 600 bucks or so. By this time, I just had a few hundred left in the bank. Somehow, I gathered 600 and paid the lawyer. We got the lawyer whose name was Yolanda. After I paid the lawyer her fee, I asked her to help me as I began to fax these offers.

She was also our escrow. I put about $1000 in the escrow and started to send these offers to the homeowners who were selling their houses. I didn't want a real estate agent for this. Many homeowners did not even consider me. Who would consider $1000 for a house?

We decided to buy under my partner's name because I just had three months in my bank account, and it was only a couple of grand. That way at least we were implementing what we learned. We started to hunt houses. In Miami, in those days the market was really awesome. This was 2005. Houses were appreciating the moment we put the offer.

We'd put an offer for 140,000 on a condo, and then we'd get back a response such as, "Sorry it's already sold, we got a cash buyer that paid $160,000 for that." We said, "But your listing price to $140,000! We're here giving you what you want, why would you sell? Is it because you got cash or because you got $20,000 more?" Well, it's an investor's market they told me. Then I sat all night and thought about how I was going to do this the right way.

This happened for a couple of deals where cash buyers just bought it, even though we made the offer. Then finally we bought this coral point. We still own that property today. Coral point, I found out, is a builder and actually works with a builder. We made the down payment, and we were able to finance it together.

My partner was only six or seven months into working at that time. He didn't have much of the money, and we thought that the builder would pay the closing cost. That's the understanding for a new development. With the down payment, we prolonged the closing date for about 45 days to 60 days. We prolonged it by paying the high-interest rate and then we purchase that property. That's how we purchased the first property and made our first investment.

Through this story, I want people to really understand that you have to see the opportunity with the way. And that's when you have to take action. You did the work. You did the research. And you acted. There are opportunities in every market and every economy, and it's up to you to find the action step that you want to take and to do it. There is no such thing as a right time or a wrong time. It is just a person's view of what's happening around them. If they watch it closely, they can find that every time is the right time for something.

Chapter 2: Purify Your Mind and Body

I will start this chapter with a story, about a man named Srinivas Raju. Srinivas was born very pure. He had taken different messages and information all around him from the people that he came across. He assimilated the information based on other people's individual experiences and viewpoints that he had seen happening from his own eyes.

This is the technique that only lets you look ahead but not inward. Srinivas was always trying to purify his mind. He felt that if he purified his mind and kept it open, in order to take new information without any bias and process it unbiased, he could just transform his entire life. His life was built upon the view that he had from his childhood till adulthood. But what if that view changed?

There used to be an old saying that if you change the way you look at things, that thing changes. In the same way, if Srinivas is able to purify his mind, which is the number one tool that has been given to us by God, he will be able to view the same situation differently. This gives him an added advantage: the power to make tough decisions that are necessary for him to transform his life. Just like Tony Robbins always said, most of the people want to make the right decision, so they make no decision, which is a decision. That's acting through autopilot. You're just going forward with all the information gathered, with no compass.

However, if you are able to see that you are a creative power, then you can decide at every moment of life the direction in which you are going. The first thing to do is to analyze where you are and know where you're headed to. If you go off-course, you just turn back and go towards that destination. If Srinivas is able to purify his mind, what happens is it becomes a new instrument, which has clarity in it. And since the mind is also compared to a muscle, the more he works on it, the better he can get at looking at the situation as it is, not as he feels it is. Then he can make decisions that can take him towards his destination. That's how it works with the mind.

Now, since there are two parts to the entire system, there's also a body associated, a physical body associated with this mind. As the old saying goes, a sound body is a sound mind. Just having a strong mind without a strong body for it to live in it is really impossible, purifying the body is equally important. The system works this way. Srinivas starts with the mind, and then he focuses on purifying his body by having an excellent diet and a rigorous exercise routine, and this, in turn, would feed into strengthening his mind and purifying it even further. And as that cycle continues, he becomes stronger, both inwardly as well as outwardly.

The inner world that he has would slowly start reflecting outside. That is if he's happy on the inside. If the chemicals produced by his body are also supporting it, automatically he can produce happy conditions outside. That's because he will choose those activities that would make him happy, which will then bring him the results he wants.

Now, most people choose activities that are convenient. Some people choose to smoke because it feels good. But it is detrimental to their health. As time goes by, they become addicted to smoking, and then they lose their health. Their mind stops deciding. Their minds have no will, no power of its own. It just becomes a lazy mind or a weak mind, and with that, their bodies also lose the power. Taking steps to purify the mind is the first step.

Purifying an inner world is nothing other than feeling peaceful. Most people want to go after peace as if it's a final destination, but peace is a basic requirement of life. If we understand that, and these two steps are taken and practiced, automatically people will be peaceful from the inside. Being peaceful means nothing else but a calm mind, a powerful mind that is able to take the necessary decisions and direct their body as well as other people to go in the right direction.

This means taking the road that would take people to the destination of prosperity, which is what everyone wants, including Srinivas. Everyone listens to the key to success. I believe the key to success is provided at birth. However, in order to open the door of success, you need energy, counsel of where the door is, and also the knowledge that you have a key. With these three elements, all you have to do is pick up the key and then put it in the door and open it to success. That's the simple step to success.

However, most people miss the part of picking up the key, which is the action. They like to have the knowledge. They'd like to have a support system. They know they have the key, but even then, they fail to take action. If they can get these four important steps aligned, they can open the door of success for themselves.

One day, when all my friends were studying, and I was studying as well, there was one gentleman who had used an influence. What I mean by influence is, he knew somebody who knew the person was giving them a job, and he got a job. This gentleman got that job, and then he told everybody he got the job, he felt successful. However, he had no skill. I felt that he did not deserve the job, because he didn't have the adequate aptitude, but he got it because of his connection.

Then looking at him, a lot of people started reading – they did not have influence, so they decided to read. What I did instead was I started applying to jobs as if I had influence, which I didn't, and I did get a job interview. When I went to the interview, they looked at me; I had rented a suit from one of my friends, Jack, and it was an Armani suit.

They said, "We like what you have, all the information that you have provided about your background and everything, but we think you'd fit in the field." At the time, although I didn't have any money, I rejected that job. I did that because that's not the line I wanted to take. More importantly, I rejected it because I had to decide. I had to feel that I still had a choice.

When I rejected the job, I became as equally famous as that other gentleman in our group who got the job with influence. People came up to me and said, "How did you reject the job? They were ready to give you a job, and you rejected." They were so surprised because there was a recession at that time, and I was the only one who got a job. I said, "I feel that I have a choice." But deep down, I was unhappy. That's when I started working out. However, my combination was "eat the pizza and then go to work out." Still, I felt better than most people.

At that time, I had gone to work out because it was free in the college gym, and everybody started telling me, "Oh, you rejected a job," and I needed to kind of feel better. I did not have the awareness that working out can help you make proper decisions, but that's how my workout journey started. I had an argument with my business partner at that time.

I told him, "Money is everything." He told me, "No. Your physical body and fitness are everything." And then he argued, "If you had a great body, you could make a lot of money." I told him, "If you have a lot of money, you can really have a great body." Our argument was about education versus fitness.

For a major part of my early life, I had the belief that money was everything. It was because my mother had told me at a young age that money is very important. I always thought, "Money is the way to go." Then after the breakthrough that I had after that job that I rejected, I just flipped my belief onto what my friend and business partner had told me. "How about I do fitness instead of going after money?" That's how I kept myself fit, by working out time and time again, but regularly.

I started feeling energetic and just better overall, which is wealth in itself. Think about it. If you had all the money in the world and you'd feel good, according to me, you have no money or wealth as you cannot enjoy spending it. I remember a friend of mine back in India, who had become a priest for the Catholic Church, had told me that the body is a gift given to us by God, and we have no right to violate it with drinks or smoking.

Back then, I'd said to him, "You're a priest, and that's your way of talking, but I'm enjoying smoking. I want to keep doing what I have to do." It was much later that I realized what he said is the truth. Your body is the only place you have to live anyway so if you take good care of it, then not only can you serve yourselves, but you can also serve others in need. There's nothing that can give you more happiness than being of value to another human being or creature on this earth. That's when true happiness comes.

It's in our best interests to realize everything is important, even something as small as the little finger, that we don't give a lot of value to. That's what I tell my team members at work. Imagine a day when your little finger stopped moving. That would be the worst day. I believe we should be grateful for all the things we already have.

We were born rich, and it's up to us to grow and keep it that way and get wealthier. That's why purifying the mind, and the body is important. It is what would help people realize what's most important for them. It may not be solving that computer code or project. It may not even be making more money. What's the most important thing that can give them the inner peace, inner calmness? It's the training of the mind, purifying and training of the mind.

Chapter 3: Increase Your Value

Now that you have learned how important purifying your body is and now that you are committed to it, you know that you can have more health, more clarity, and more energy. You can apply that energy to become better at your career and life in general. You can use it to increase your value. In other words, you can use it to increase your bill rate or salary.

I went through this in a slightly different way. I observed successful people not just for one day, or for two days, but for several years. I just observed and made notes of all the successful people that I knew of personally at that time. What is it that they were doing that I could do at that time? What is it that they did that I mustn't do when I get to where they are at, financially and otherwise? At that point, I just felt financial success to be very important.

However, to balance that out, I also knew that I could only be happy with integrity, and not just financial success.

You won't believe the number of successful people, in India particularly, that are fed with the information that success only comes to you when you are evil. That is simply not true. Success comes when you have integrity.

What is important to people? It can be increasing their bill rate or the stability of their job that already provides them a certain level of financial success. How can they find out what matters to them? They can only be clear about it once they purify their mind and body. When their mind and body are pure, they can see the situation as it really is. Their decision about increasing their bill rate, or increasing their value at wherever they're working at, can only be right if they make it with a clear mind.

Consider increasing your bill rate. This can happen in two ways. One, you can increase your bill rate at the same project where you work at present; you can do this by becoming invaluable to the client or employer. And two, you can find another project or job with a different client, someone who is willing to pay more for your services. Your big goal of increased value is decided by the client. It is also determined by the complexity of the job. In this way, you can make sure the value provided is paid for.

There was a person who had worked with me for almost six years. Let's call him Roy. When he joined our company, his bill rate was $55 an hour. He moved projects at $55, $45, $47. Because of mainframes technology, he moved to various clients, but the bill rate remained low. Now, he provided value to the clients in mainframes technology. However, the marketplace didn't value the solution that he provided – that is, mainframes, an antiquated technology by then and something not trainable for other people.

Since not many clients used that technology anymore, Roy was just stuck at the low bill rate. One day, I had a conversation with him in which I explained to him that new people, new graduates, who have far less experience than him were making almost double his bill rate. How did they do that? It's because they were providing solutions to the clients in big data, cloud, and Hadoop – all new technologies clients were using. Roy was fascinated.

He took that information to his heart and started learning at night. He learned big data solutions, and in a matter of two or three years, his bill rate had grown to $100 plus per hour. As of this year, his bill rate was around $140 per hour. He made that leap within the span of six years. To transform your life, you have to reframe. Change your perspective by asking yourself the right questions. Ask yourself, "What type of life do I want?" Answering that question will bring you clarity not only about your goals but also how you are going to achieve them. And then when you transform it, you will feel accomplished. Contrary to popular belief, not many people ask themselves this question that is so vital for success.

Increasing your bill rate doesn't mean your life is going to magically become simple. There is a possibility that you might have to work harder, put in more time. However, if that is what you really want, then you will walk the extra mile for your success. As you do that, you will realize that you are ready to do what it takes. Programming yourself for success will take some time, but you can do it.

This is how it works: your output depends on the input. If you feed your brain discouraging tales of how you can't do it then, of course, you won't be able to. Your brain works just like a computer. Consider your brain as the hard drive of your system — the rules of programming work when it comes to your brain. If you enter negativity, then negative outcomes are what you will get. Programming yourself for success will take time and effort.

Take control of your thoughts. Make your thoughts positive and affirmative so that your actions correspond to your thoughts. For this process to become programmed into your system, you have to repeat it over and over again till it becomes your autopilot. Success begins when you take the first step to change your mindset. You might not have been trained for success. Take my example; I didn't have the rich dad advice in my life. However, I didn't let that stop me.

I reprogrammed myself so that I would go for success without letting doubts stop me. In other words, you have to reprogram your mind to aim high. People will tell you to set tiny goals and to attain them one by one so that success comes incrementally to you. However, don't let that stop you from setting big goals for yourself. Go all out. Retrain your brain so that success doesn't seem like an impossible ambition to you anymore.

Reinforce the thought in your brain that you can do whatever you set your mind to; in time, you will get there. As the habit of success is cemented in your mind through reprogramming, succeeding will become second nature to you. You wouldn't think twice about it because success will come naturally to you. Remember, it will happen only if you program yourself for it. After all, what have you got to lose but the habit of losing?

Chapter 4: Location Aligned With Destiny

Now that you have learned to increase your bill rate, it is time for you to look at the best place to maximize your value. You may have several offers to go to a place where you will have more value. However, you might still turn those opportunities away. Why? You might not have the mental clarity to appraise prospects clearly. You have to be in the right mental state to be able to focus. In other words, you have to be focused on aligning your location with your destiny.

I have seen many people who align themselves with their location in different ways. Consider the example of a married man with children. Now, his priorities in life are only to look at the best interest for his family mostly children. He filters his opportunities by asking how it would benefit his children or his family. Sometimes what happens is that he will put his family in one location and he will go off and work elsewhere. That's the sacrifice that he makes for the better future of his kids. He would travel back and forth on an expense paid project or a project that does not reimburse travel expenses. That way his children can go to great schools, and he can travel and come back. My own father did something like this.

Now, that's a great sacrifice in my opinion because that way children get a good education and the father is able to get what you call another location. This is another location where the father found a good opportunity, and he took it without making any compromises. I can't impose a single method for everybody; however, what is common between people is the way they can navigate through it all.

Consider the example of possibly learning a new skill that is highly profitable. Now, what I have seen it happen a lot is that most people fail to realize the profit they can have by learning a new skill. They can literally add their years of experience to the knowledge that they have just accumulated.

For example, someone who has been in IT for about 10 years spends three weeks on learning a new technology like big data or Artificial Intelligence. He does this for a period of two to three weeks. Once he learns this skill, he can apply for the jobs or projects with an understanding that he now has 10 years and 3 weeks of experience in technology. However, unfortunately the marketplace doesn't pay for the years of experience in the other technologies that he has for some new technology that he has just learned.

What can he do now? He can come up with a relatively reasonable salary for the new technology that he has learned so that it benefits him/her in the long run. Here is the lesson you can learn from this example: the marketplace pays for the value you bring to the marketplace, not for the years of experience that the immigrant, the consultant or the IT worker has, or any person has or had in the past. If you understand this simple concept, you can make use of any new skills you learn.

You can actually serve a few clients, gain the understanding and experience and then proceed from there. Now naturally due to the years of experience and understanding of the systems behind it, you will gain the understanding in a fairly shorter timeframe than someone who just started to learn these new technologies. This means you might have to serve the customer with a lower bill rate initially, to gain further knowledge and conquer different industries that you want, which the customer will expose you to. It is possible you can obtain a higher rate right from the beginning of the search as it depends on the technology and the client's needs.

For example, if you are working in the retail industry, you will have customers whose business problems you solve. You can serve any customer in that industry, but to gain an in-depth understanding, you should have the right focus and a willingness to go the extra mile in learning what their needs are. To get the right customers, you will probably get a project with a lower bill rate initially. Once you gain further understanding, which will be fairly quick, you can obtain a higher billing or charge more.

You will be able to do that because you have more knowledge than any new worker who just got trained. You might have to make a little bit of sacrifice, by either lowering the bill rate or, in some cases, having a higher bill rate than what you are already making but one that is still lower for that technology. That is a strategy which you can use.

In other words, you make decisions after looking at the overall picture. You have to ask yourself the question, "Where can I bring the most value?" When there are new developments in technology or in your industry, you can make the decisions accordingly. If it is worth it to lower your bill rate for some time to get access to that knowledge until you become an expert at it, you will make the tough decision to do that. This isn't something that many people would do as they will consider it from a limited perspective.

However, when you do that, you know you will be one of the few people who have that niche knowledge. Ultimately, your decision will increase your value, and you go back to your higher bill rate in time. The key is choosing the right technology. That's where a lot of people make mistakes. For example, a new technology comes into the market; they realize that a lot of people are getting trained and they get trained without adequate research in that technology.

However, it is important to know that if technology is going to be sustainable for a longer period of time. Research will ensure that you have a stable project. And you can work for a long-term while at the same time have a higher bill rate. You look at the long-term, but at the same time, you don't forget that this is about the location.

Now some people might feel that a higher rate is not

their goal. They might say, "Why would I need a higher rate? I just need to be stable!" This is the mentality that some people have. There is nothing wrong with that mentality but the situation in the United States is that it is a fast-moving country and fast-moving economy. If you want to be stable, the best way to do it is by building more and more knowledge. In the field of business, there is an old saying: "Either you're growing, or you're dying."

The same applies to the job market. If you are not developing new skills, you will become antiquated. There will come a time when you might find yourself out of opportunities and jobs, only because you did not invest in learning and increasing your value. The immigrants on a work visa are in the country on purpose because of the highly specialized skills they bring to the marketplace. In order to comply with that original reason that they are on a visa to make more sense for the country to have them, they should constantly provide more value than anyone else.

That should be your motto. Stability is viewed by many as being stable in one location. When they are settled in one location, they have financial comfort, and that's stability to them. However, after some time as things change, they will not have enough financial resources in order to sustain their stability. The reasons are the changing economy. You have got to keep growing to maintain your stability in the country.

You need to always increase your value so that you are always in abundance. As the world around you continues to have inflation, this is the only way you can ensure your spot at the top of that curve. When you notice that your bill rate is going down, it is up to you to go to look for new skills and new opportunities that the market is offering. The bill rate is a direct reflection of the value or perceived value that you bring to the marketplace. You have to always be in touch with your market, is because the market determines your value.

You have to analyze the market and understand where it sees value. And then, you need to align your value with the location that the market determines to be valuable. Value is not determined with the individual or the expert. Value is determined by the market. Knowing your market and marketing is one of the highest skill-sets you can ever have.

What are the ways that you can determine value? For example, you provide service to a particular customer; you have to see the total value that you contribute to your customer. Suppose there is a project that pays X number of dollars per hour. Most of the consultants and IT workers will work to fill in the hour, and just calculate their checks for the work that they did. However, the client at the end of the month or the end of the quarter looks at the total investment that they made on the various IT workers. They will see whether the investment resulted in cost savings or efficiency in their process. It is the return on investment on the cost that shows how much is saved or how much more efficient the processes have become.

If the IT worker gains the understanding of what is valuable to the customer, they can increase the value that they are providing as a support to the customer beyond their regular consultative Information Technology expertise. And that increases the likelihood of the customer retaining them as a long-term team member for them. They believe that the IT worker is reliable, and they can depend on them to work on multiple projects in the future.

On the other hand, if the IT worker just works and performs and provides technical expertise to the customer, and then just collects the check, once the project is complete the customer no longer has any interest to retain the temporary IT worker that they hired to begin with. That would be the end of the project for him even though he provided good service.

As an example, for the first case scenario, let me tell you the story of this one gentleman I knew of. Sai was working as a network engineer at one of our clients. At the end of the project, the client was so impressed that they didn't want to let him go even though they did not have any further work for him in the same location.

However, the manager felt like this gentleman had provided tremendous value, so they referred him to other locations. They gave him another project in their Ohio branch upon completion of his New Jersey Project, and after that was over, they retransferred him back to New York City and then back to New Jersey. He ended up working three years for that client just because he had provided more value and they believed that he was a stable resource that they could count on.

You can benefit by demonstrating that you can bring more value to your client. Take the steps today so you can reap the rewards in your future.

Chapter 5: Financial Awareness

The first day I went to work I wanted to get a sports car for myself. I was walking out of the parking lot, where I saw all the cars. Naturally, I wanted to have one for myself. I just looked at one very nice car that was there and keeping that in mind, I started going to work each and every day with the thought that I would save some money, and then apply for financing and buy the car.

Somewhere down the line, when I was ready to buy the Jeep Wrangler, which was and still is my favorite car, I found that the monthly payment for it was about $350 if I put $2,000 down. With the financing, I could get that car. Just when I got ready to purchase the car, I lost my job. You'd think that would change my mind immediately. However, that's not what happened. I was still very, very tempted to go and purchase the car despite the fact that I had lost my job. I thought, "Okay. I'm going to do it anyway. It's a pre-approved. Let me just get the car that I want." I even took my friend's car for a ride, and then I was ready to go get my car. In the evening, I decided, "No. I'm so broke. Let me wait until I can get this car. That's the dream car that I really want."

At the same time, one of my bosses needed some help with a computer, so I went to fix it for him. I got a temporary job for a couple of days. As I was fixing his home computer, he asked me, "How are things going on? I know you just lost your job." I said, "Yeah. It's been tough. I want to buy this car." I explained to him the car agreement and how much I wanted to get it. He was a Finance Director of the company that I used to work for. He said to me, "Why would you want to buy a car? A car depreciates, whereas if you buy a house, it will appreciate."

I asked, "What does appreciate mean? I appreciate living in a home." He said, "No, no, no. That's not what it is. Appreciate means that a house increases in value." Then that's when I began to understand what an asset is. He explained to me that an asset is something that you own which increases in value or generates income. On the other hand, liability is something which has monthly payments or one huge payment or an expense that we have to pay to somebody else. I started to understand that the car would be a liability. Why would I go after the car, something that takes us from point A to point B? It would depreciate, which means I would lose money without doing anything. At that time, I decided, "Okay. Instead of the car, I'm going to go and buy a house." That's how I changed my view.

I went and read the book *Rich Dad, Poor Dad* by Robert Kiyosaki, and I began to understand more about assets and liabilities. In the book, the author shows a Cashflow Quadrant which is divided in this way: employee, self-employed, business owner, and investor. The author explains that most people in America are on the left side of the quadrant. They are either employees or self-employed. That means they trade time for money. The business owners and investors are on the right side of the quadrant; they actually own more than half of the country's wealth. Get this: one percent of people own more than half of the country's wealth. That's the statistic.

I was so fascinated with the entire idea that I wanted to understand finance in more detail. That's when I started to learn more about finance along with IT. No matter what our profession is, we have to have basic financial education to make money for ourselves.

I made a very important, but also very funny, move after this. I bought an old Lincoln car for $400 instead of a Jeep just to keep the expenses low. I knew that there's no way that Lincoln would depreciate beyond the $400. I had the Lincoln. It ran about for six months until it broke, but within that period I got back on track and found a different job.

Most of the H1-B visa holders and immigrants who are here for work in the US make a lot of sacrifices to come here. They leave their families and loved ones. In some cases, they may not even visit back home for several years. In that process, why wouldn't they want to trade that sacrifice for growing in their career? It is what they are here for. The immigrants believe that they are actually going to earn more money. Some of them feel that they are going to earn money and then go back to their native countries. Some decide that they are going to earn money and live permanently in the States.

As they come along the first job and they see their paychecks coming in, they immediately decide, "Now I'm making money. I'm on my own feet here, I got to improve my standard of living." About 70-80% of them go and buy a BMW car or any other luxury car because that's the car that's known to be prestigious in most of these other countries. With financing, they get a BMW. They buy this car just to show to the rest of the world that they're doing well.

What happens is that they coast along for a few months where the car takes away more payments. After a couple of years, some of them decide, "I'm going to buy a property back in my home country." That's what some of my friends did. They bought properties and lands in India while they were working in the US. It was smart because they had some rental income coming in. But in most cases, the rental income does not match the price that they spent on the land. They have to send the money for the mortgage, so hoping the land will appreciate.

Some the immigrants follow this path where they buy some property, a rental property or land, without realizing that doing so only increases their own liability. It's an additional expense, and they don't count that. They just coast along with this increasing their assets outside the US. Now most of them don't realize that as they're doing it, even if they have income outside of the US, even though they're not a US Citizen, yet they still have to report taxes in the US.

It's a good idea to check with our accountant about taxes by paying their fees. Some of the others have so many properties outside the US that their primary idea of living in the US just fades away because they need to go back, which is again going to interfere with their aim of being a person of great value or their aim of living in the United States. They are going where the wind blows rather than being self-directed and going towards their destination.

Napoleon Hill's Think and Grow Rich says, "If you want to find the treasure, you have to burn the boat." You should make the decision of whether you want to stay here or leave the country. If you decide that you're going to stay temporary, have a definite date within which you will provide valuable service, learn technologies and new ideas of innovation. Then go back and start your own businesses or pursue a career which you are passionate about in your home country3.

If you have an unclear vision, you are just going to play along. You'll say, "Let's see what happens next year. Let's see what's going to be the new rules that's going to come across ten years from now? Right now, it's so volatile, the market. I don't know if the recession is going to be nearby. I better leave now." This isn't wise. You should make long term strategies. In order to be financially successful in the States, your assets and income should be greater than your liabilities. That's the first financial tip I would give.

A friend of mine and the previous mentor once told me that, "Vijai, as you go along and get richer and richer, do not increase your liability beyond $70K job." I asked him, "Why would you say that?" He said, "The reason you don't have increased beyond the $70K job is if all else fails, and the market crashes, you can still get a $70K job. Then you can still manage the same type of lifestyle that you've been living without completely breaking down." I said, "But you are a multimillionaire, and you have a three-million-dollar property. Why are you talking about the $70K?"

Then he explained, "Even though I have a three-million-dollar property, with all the taxes and everything I've already paid in cash, my liability does not exceed the $70K." I understood what he was saying, and his advice has served me very well since. We all want things to be sunny all the time, but the recession is coming, and it's a great time to read this book and take action. I have been through two recessions in the United States. Recession typically occurs when people are not spending, currencies are devalued, war, government instability, rising interest rates, and various other reasons.

Consumer spending decreases, and there is inflation particularly because of rising interest rates, rising home prices, or anything that has artificially increased in value. The market will correct itself, and that's going to disrupt the entire financial system. That leads to recession. What's common in all of the recessions is that there is a limited number of jobs. Consumers will not be spending more money, which is going to affect businesses. Some of the people would lose jobs. Some would lose businesses. Also, businesses will stop investing in human resources because it is a big expense.

They would start investing in innovative technologies that can work without people. In that process, they would have to lay off any foreign worker first. Anybody on a visa would be laid off first. Then they would lay off the green card holders, a permanent resident. Green card holders are immigrants still on visa though it is a permanent visa.

With this kind of situation, the H1-B workers who have been working on permanent employment with various big companies are suddenly going to be laid off, given a severance and asked to either leave the country or find employment elsewhere if they wish to continue. That's a very important factor to consider. As an IT Consultant, we know the complexity of work that's being performed, and so we all tend to feel, "I am a key resource of the project. They're not going to terminate me. I'm a key resource because I can do the work of three other consultants."

However,, when it comes to finance, they're going to see differently. They might even decide they don't need the project that you are working on. If they believe that they can stall the project until their revenue or capital position or profit increases, they will lay off the technical resource.

This applies to employees across the board. Technical people think that their value is the technology that they bring to the table. However, the technology adopted by the company, in some cases, is a nice-to-have more than a need-to-have thing. Often, one of the first departments to be affected is the technology department, where massive layoffs occur.

There're only two purposes for an employee in the company. The first one is either they bring in the revenue, or they cut cost. Now cutting cost can go into further if you can classify it as operational efficiency or HR workflow management. Or they're in sales and marketing and bringing in the revenue. With that said, if they're the technical person providing technology, they're for the cost-cutting part of it mostly unless they're building platforms that can improve the business sales, or the marketing division providing technical solutions for marketing. It is a good idea for the consultant or the IT worker to understand the true value that they are providing. A good way is to look at their own metrics, of what the company has given them.

Let's say they completed a project in three months, and then they can compare the salary they got for the three months and see, "Did it contribute to cutting any cost at all for the company, or did it increase the overall efficiency for the stakeholders of the project, or it's going to be another three months before they really realize that this work was worth it?" If they view it from the customer end standpoint, they will benefit.

They also need to keep an eye on where the company is headed. If the company is at a loss, it's just a matter of time after some time that, if the efficiency is not being realized, they'll scrap the entire project. With better awareness, you can make better choices. With better choices, you can get better results. This was a quote by one of my first mentors, Robin Sharma. These financial tips will help any consultant build awareness.

To reach your destination, you have to know two things. One, where you are. Two, where you want to be. If you don't know where you are, then wherever you go will not likely be the place that you want to be. This book will give you an awareness of where you currently stand, what are your true dreams and goals, and the commitment that you have to make in order to pass through the recession or pass through your career with the maximum achievement possible for you as an individual.

Depending on the nature of the IT worker or technological expertise, it may just make sense that when the recession hits, they just leave the country and come back later after the recession. That may be an option. This would give them a compass on where they are. Then they can analyze what's the external condition that they have to keep an eye on. Don't pay attention to the news whether it is real news or fake news. Just pay attention to the internal factors that will determine your success and the outside conditions.

In the recession of 2008, most testers likely lost their jobs. The only people that had jobs were highly skilled SAP consultants, Java developers, and a few others. These were the only few consultants who made it through the recession. Granted their bill rates were not that high because consumer spending is low, and the business spending was also at an all-time low. But they did make it through the recession because those technologies did thrive through the recession.

I'm not saying that those are the same technologies that'll be thriving through this coming recession. However, to understand what type of projects that many clients are working on, you have to ask, "Are those projects need-to-have projects?" In other words, it is very important to map out that the type of projects that you have worked on, or you can work on as an IT worker, are need-to-have or not. Find out how many of them are need-to-have. Once that is identified, you know which areas you have to strengthen within your experience and knowledge.

Additionally, make sure that you are able to provide the clients with insights on how they can further cut their costs. As an IT worker and consultant, we all feel, "Hey, I did a great job! Then I have worked 18 hours. I completed this project, and I put in 18 hours a day for almost three months. Last three months I didn't sleep at all, and I finished my projects by the deadline." However, through that process, just remember, if you can also cut the client's cost, they will view you as an investment, not an expense. This is a soft skill that is missed by many technical consultants.

Let's talk about tax breaks on housing now from an immigrant perspective. What are the opportunities that you have when a recession hits? You're not allowed to start a business in the United States. However, one of the reasons someone wants to start businesses in the United States is they want to actually create jobs, they want to have tax benefits. And they want to be able to have passive income or active income from their own enterprise. However, you cannot start a business because you are an immigrant. But can you buy a property? The answer is yes.

Now, most of the immigrants that buy a property want to live in it. The problem with that kind of an arrangement is if you buy a property to live in it, you'll be paying the mortgage. The mortgage doesn't stop during a recession. They may get some tax benefits, but that's about it. And if something happens during the recession, they will be forced to sell their properties and leave the United States. If not that then they will be forced to sell their properties and move into smaller rental properties.

I personally had two rental properties that I had interest in. It was generating the rental income despite the recession. One of the strategies that you can adopt is to buy a rental property, and then rent it out to the State in which you reside. If you are able to rent a property to the State, as long as the State does not default which is usually the case, there is a guaranteed ACH credit every month into your bank account. If you make a proper investment, you will have a guaranteed cash flow during a recession.

A friend of mine bought five properties. Each were worth $70,000. He fixed them. All were with mortgages. He did not buy $70,000 in cash, but he paid more interest because it's less than $100,000. But he fixed those properties and then rented it out to State. Overall, he was making about $2,500 positive cash flow through that process. Different states have a voucher program. A simple Google search for voucher programs within your State would allow you to reach out to the Housing Authority in your area.

Talk to them about the areas in which they're promoting

the voucher program. This way, you can have a steady income during a recession. If you are already in foreclosure, you can negotiate with the bank. If the bank allows, then they can definitely go for it. You can negotiate anything in real estate. Bank needs their money; They do not want the property. If the negotiations make sense, the bank would agree.

Another thing that you should understand is 401(k). In simple words, 401(k) is a retirement savings plan which your employer sponsors. With this plan, you can save as well as invest a part of your paycheck before the deduction of taxes. Until you withdraw money from your account, taxes won't be paid.

Then you must also understand compound interest. Let's use an example to understand this concept. A person who is 20 years of age makes a $5,000 investment. By the time they are 65, they would have close to $140,000 in their account. That is if there are no bank fees. In other words, that's called the power of compounding. Most of the immigrants think that the 401K is not a great investment for them because they're not sure if they're going to stay in the country or leave after a few years.

However, if they make the decision to stay, and they're committed to this plan, then investing in the 401(k). is a very, very wise investment. It's because 401(k) is a tax-deferred plan. With a 401(k) investment, you can get some money towards your savings and investments. Most employers offer 401(k). Even so, immigrants do not capitalize on that. They feel if they invest in it, their money will be gone forever. But I suggest investing in 401(k) and review strategies with your accountant as you generate income. If you can save some tax dollars, it is a worthy investment. If you stay long enough, you will get returns on your investment.

In order for you to have better finances, you have to understand the language of finance. The words that are used will determine your financial wellbeing. If you use positive words – for example, if you say, "We sold the stock. We had some profit" – then those are the type of things that will come into your life. Financial success is only built on success.

Start slowly with financial success. You can start with saving, and then slowly take bold moves in investing. Most of the people think that they can save their way to retirement. Unfortunately, retirement is very close. By that time, many of you would already get the green card and become citizens. You will retire very quickly. To make the decision of a small disciplined investment will create financial success for you far quicker than if you waited until becoming a green card holder or a citizen. Make the move now, if you haven't already.

Chapter 6: Give First Mentality

What does it take to have a give first mentality? You have already learned about increasing your value and making wise investments in yourself and in your future. Now you have to look beyond it. It means you have to look past your personal interests and stop thinking about what you can get. Instead, start thinking about what you can give.

Have you ever thought about how you can give billions back?

It is very interesting when people get their first paycheck. They graduate and get their first job; looking at the paycheck; they decide, "I have to see more of this." That's where wanting more begins. My first paycheck was $60. Like many other people, I thought to myself, "Hey, I'm working!" With most people, though, what happens is that they just think they have to work. The list includes me as well., We think we have to work and get paid. This goes on and, on. Eventually, people see that they need to get paid more doing the same thing.

Unfortunately, what happens is they get to a point where that doesn't seem to happen for them. They keep doing the same thing, and so they keep getting the same paycheck that they always have. One of two things can happen at that point. One, they decide, "What am I doing that's not increasing this pay?" Two, "That's the way the world works." People who choose the second option then go on to live their lives just in that way; they just get the raises that may be adjusted or slightly adjusted based on inflation, but it is not on par with the society that moves forward at a high speed.

I remember when I was in that situation, I called my dad and just said to him, "Hey dad, I'm making $800 a month, right? My tuition is being paid off because of scholarship and all the other stuff. I'd like to be a student forever. I'm still able to save $200; I don't need more money. I don't need any more money. I'm doing happy," I said those things not because they were true – which they were – but because I felt beaten up by the whole system that stipulates you can only work on campus. That's what I was doing.

You know what my dad said to me? He told me the story where of a pig which was in very, very, dirty water. The pig was happy thinking that's life. The human being that stood outside the pond said, "That's a dirty pond. Well, that's dirty water." My dad just ended the story and left it at that. And I started thinking, "Wow, he just called me a pig!" What happened was, I was able to make ends meet, but I was unable to see I could do so much more.

My way of thinking changed after that. I began to ask myself, "Why am I getting paid only so much?" And the answer that I received was, "Okay it's not the hours that I'm working. It's what I'm giving back to the employer." The desk job that I was working during day shift paid me $6 an hour. As a desk attendant, you swipe the IDs, and let the people into the dorm rooms.

That's what my job was. And interestingly, I decided, "How do I increase the value that I can provide to these people?" I analyzed other people that were doing the same work that I was but might be paid more. With some research, I found that at the graveyard, they paid $8 an hour for the same job.

Then I realized that's because the work required more

effort. That area gave more money, and you had more value there because night is when they want someone to work. Anybody is available during the daytime, but at night, nobody is. I started doing that.

I realized then that giving more back, in terms of effort and the time that I worked, increased my paycheck. By being there, I was recognized as the desk attendant of the month. I felt great about it! It felt good because I was there if anybody else did not show up or could not work in the graveyard shift. I was there, ready to work that shift. I was happy not because I got the extra $2 per hour, but because of the feeling of being valued that they gave me.

I also got a $20 gift which was four hours of work. That kind of got me thinking, and I started doing more reading on what other things that we can do to give more value to others. The thing with paychecks is, you get to a point where your needs are being met with your current salary. When your salary is enough to fulfil your basic needs, that's the point that you have to be very, very careful.

That's when most people become satisfied and think, "I am doing okay." This then escalates to them thinking, "I have done enough. Nobody can tell me anything, I'm making money, I have my own car, I have my house, I take care of my family, and I've done enough." Now, according to me, that's a little bit selfish. Do you stop giving because you have done enough? You will realize that as you start giving, you will get better at it. At the same time, the marketplace is moving. You may not be watching. And whatever you have been providing is going to get lower and lower as time goes on. So, that's something to think about.

There is an old Indian adage that says: "If I am doing well I'm going to make sure that my family is doing well and then if my family and I are doing well, I can make sure that my neighbors are okay. If they're in trouble, I can help them. If I can help the neighbors, I can help the entire community, the entire district." It is through thinking this way that you can impact the whole world. And you can do that just by being helpful. If you are giving value and you are taking care of yourself as well as others, then the whole process works.

What most people do is, they only care about themselves. Unfortunately, they are the unhappiest people on earth. Despite all the things that they may do, they will face some kind of inconvenience. This is how the universe works. If you want to try this out, just try doing something for someone. It could be as simple as doing something for people you really love. For example, people work hard all their life just to make sure that their kids go to the best college they can possibly afford. They put in so much for their kids' education. That's their kid's life or, in other cases, their spouse's life or their parents' life. And just thinking about doing something for someone that they love increases their energy.

You may be doing this even now. If you have already helped your loved ones, then are you ready to take the extra step? This is the time that you step into the realm of the universe. Now, the value that you are going to provide is no longer about yourself. That's what will take you to a whole new level of human satisfaction and bliss. You get to that level because your life is no longer just about you. It is about the whole universe as one whole element of which you are a part.

As you increase your value, you are actually asking the universe to work through you to help others. People who chase money are never fulfilled by money alone. But if you chase the question of how you can create more value, help more people, serve your family, community and even humanity as a whole, it will bring you the contentment that you need. This is what will expand you so that you become a vessel that the universe is working through. Money then is the result of the value that you create for other people. As you do that, you will no longer get stuck in the trap of thinking that your paycheck is your value. Your paycheck is not your value. It is what you serve, how you serve, the skills that you provide, and who you serve, that is your true value.

I started to think about value when I first questioned why I was getting paid only these $6 and $8 per hour. A very simple answer came to me. That's because the skill level required to do that job is not very high. It's not a highly skilled job. Anybody with limited skills can be a desk attendant. And the errors that are done by a desk attendant are mostly forgiven. There's less risk in the job, so the errors are okay.

I mean, if you forgot to swipe someone and two people went in, there's no penalty for doing that. And even if you show up late, you're just going to lose $2-$3 for being late for half an hour. There is value, but it's not high. I understood the perceived value you provide is not the hours that you work; it's the impact that you do to an organization or a person.

Let me share a personal story where my business partner and I had an argument once where I said, "Money is everything" while he said, "No, education is everything." It was the year 2001 or 2002. It was still a recession time. My business partner had graduated by then, and I was still in college. He was looking for a job. One day, he came to me and said, "I'm going to get this Oracle DBA Certification." I asked, "How much is it?" He said, "It's like $150 bucks, and it's about six certifications or $600 or $900 for the whole certification."

I told him, "You just spent close to a $100,000 on this master's degree, and you think a regular certification is going to help? I think education is nothing. We are still working at our $6 an hour and $8 an hour jobs, and I don't think education is anything. It's all about the money. That's why we studied, right?" We had a very intense argument. However, I convinced him that he does not have to take that extra course.

To make the long story short, this is the kind of feeling most people will experience during times of adversity. They will feel that they have done enough and to do anything beyond that would be a waste of time. This is the time that you have to have caution in what you are doing.

There could be a possibility that you have some things you cannot see yet. That was the message I was conveying to my business partner. So, how much sense does it make to invest in books, education and all the materials you can get and then just leave it on the shelf? That's what you call shelf-development, not self-development!

You should consider this very important factor and not fall into a trap. So, first, you have to recognize that you are gifted. Second, you have to recognize your innate talents. You have to ask yourself, "How far have I come along?" You should have an idea of that. And looking back at that, you can strengthen what you already have. This can be in the way for you to save your money and build your finances.

In this way, you can relearn what you already learned and what you are doing well already. Just relearning it one more time can strengthen it. Bruce Lee once said, "I'm not afraid of the person who knows 10,000 different kicks. I'm afraid of that person who has practiced one kick 10,000 times." If you think about it, the pieces will fall into place, and you will start to see things differently.

Earl Nightingale considered success to be the progress

of realization to a worthy ideal. If you observe the rules of giving back, you will progress in the direction that you have to progress. You will feel successful, and when you recognize yourself progressing, that will make the universe give you more success.

When it comes to success, I believe in what Dalai Lama has said, "The purpose of life is to be happy." It may sound very simple, but most people complicate it. They are happy for a moment, sad for a moment. They're angry, dissatisfied with various emotions. But if the purpose of life is to be happy, then your success is in achieving more happiness for yourself.

Yet, a lot of people who are apparently successful in the market, are unhappy because they are not living their life through their values. And one of the values that most people do not realize is that they are born good. They think that they have to be bad in order to face life. They make up the rule that 'if I'm a good person, I'll be beaten down.'

On the contrary, that might be the initial path that you may face, but if you are good, you will attain success and fulfilment with the right focus and determination. The reason you have to give back is provided to you as soon as you are born: it is the very air you breathe that makes it binding on you to give back. Once you understand it, you will realize that Giving back is nothing but being grateful for what you have already been given. Your gratitude is the only thing that is the opposite of fear; it is the only thing that can keep you going through all adverse times. You have to give back in order to be grateful to the universe.

You focus on your skills; you can ask yourself a good question, "What can I be the best at in the world?" A part of being the best means that you have passion, you have joy, you have fulfillment from creating that value for yourself as well as humanity. And unfortunately, a lot of people in business miss this very key part of asking this question. They don't realize that they have to become specialized in their field of passion to make the most out of their potential. This way, they can benefit not only themselves but also others.

When I originally came to the U.S., the green card used to be granted within a year and a half. Then 9/11 happened so it just got postponed and I got it 10 years later. In that time, I learned a lot of things about becoming specialized so that I could give back more. You need to have grit, otherwise, you will get lost in the crowd of so many other people who have the skill and the expertise to replace you. I understood these points, and so I modified my plans accordingly. My goal originally was to be a scientist in electronics. That was my original goal. However, I had to choose computer science because the marketplace only required computer science engineering degrees for sponsoring visas.

Despite my unhappiness, I had to take that move and stand and go for what's more important. And then I realized my true talent is business. In 2004, the priority dates of employment-based immigration moved back to around 1998. A lot of friends who were there with me saw that as a bad sign, and they left the U.S.

Some went to Canada because Canadian immigration was quicker, and some just went back to India. I still stayed, staying true to the original idea that the greatest country in the world is one where there is the greatest opportunity. I had faith that the universe will give to me in time. I kept that in my mind that maybe, even if it takes 10 years, I will reach the destination that I have in mind and be an instrument of service to others. As the book, The Art of War explains, sometimes the longest route is the shortest route to your destination.

I stuck to my plan and got where I am today because I didn't give up. Learning from my own experience, I can tell you that your job is to identify a long-term path for yourself. If you are not clear of the longer path, then every little change that comes will be like day trading stock, but it is your own life you are dealing with. You have to make movements which will be very stressful, but if you are a long-term investor in your own life and you can see where investing your life can take you, then you will go all the way. Your investment in your personal development, in yourself, can take you to your destination. You will win. Just like Warren Buffett said about holding stock: "My favorite holding period is forever." In my words, "My personal development time is forever."

Chapter 7: Overcome Self-Limiting Beliefs

There are some limiting beliefs which will hold you back from achieving all the success you desire. It's important to take a good look at each one of these to make sure you are aware of them. If you are experiencing them in your own reality, you need to eliminate them immediately or otherwise, they will sabotage your energy and focus. If you are not experiencing these self-limiting beliefs, then it is still important to become aware of them, so you can watch to avoid them in the future.

"I'm Opportunistic"

When many immigrants move to the United States, they are making many sacrifices. For some of them, their only identity is progress. They associate themselves with development, and in the process of evolution, they become an opportunist.

There's nothing wrong with being an opportunist, but most of them are so captivated by this feeling that they have to be an opportunist, they lose their values. The idea here is that you have to be an opportunist; however, you have to stick to your values. That's the only way you can be happy.

I genuinely believe talent is not in just being an opportunist but being an opportunist with values. If you can get those two together, then you can be successful and happy.

For example, many immigrants like to help other immigrants. When someone truly helps them, they take the help. As soon as they have a different opportunity, they take over that opportunity at the expense of the first person who initially helped them. It could be considered climbing the ladder to success, but it is a short-sighted viewpoint. They are losing the relationship in that process. They're looking in their own selfish best interest without thinking of helping everyone and making it a win-win situation.

They are looking for a better deal at the expense of others. To look for a better deal at the expense of others is not necessarily a very nice thing. They can search for a better opportunity and progress by helping the other person who initially supported them.

That's what I'm talking about in terms of keeping their values. They know that it could be wrong, but they still do it because of their association with an identity of progress. They forget that they still have to keep their values and integrity.

They will get farther in the long run if they follow this model of keeping their values along the way of climbing the ladder of success.

Someone is only going to remain successful if, at the end of that opportunity, as the journey progresses along, the person is happy. If they're unhappy, they would be the cause of their failure. Even though they show they're successful to the rest of the world, internally, they would be a failure or feel like one.

Success on the outside doesn't last unless there is happiness on the inside as well. Whatever reflects externally, it's just a matter of time before the truth comes out. Let's keep our values while we become successful and happy.

Their happiness will make others more content, and it's a whole happy environment they're creating around them. Like the saying goes, "Like attracts like." When you are a happy and successful person, you will attract more and everlasting success. You draw more success with happiness.

Happiness is one of my secret sauces for success in my career. People want to work with happy people. They want to work with happy people because happy people truly want to help others succeed without a hidden agenda. When you feel the intention coming from another person is to help others, you can just feel it. No external reinforcement is required.

Cheating Mentality

The movies in India and many movies throughout the ages, even in the United States, have shown big-time CEOs and big-time company owners in business as a stereotype that they're all cheats. Where many artists give their sweat and blood, these big business CEOs exploit them and then profit on their sacrifices to become more productive and richer.

With this thought process, many of the immigrants when they initially come to the US have a feeling that they have to cheat to become rich. They think they have to protect themselves, and therefore also cheat. We call it an opportunity by cheating, but that is a temporary opportunity which doesn't last forever.

The cheating mentality is the root cause of the failure of many immigrants. If someone can overcome that destructive mentality, they will have a chance at lasting success in the United States. They need to be clear about who they are at their core values and feel for what they are at their highest integrity. They're not cheaters. They're good people.

If you can overcome this brainwashing that movies have placed into your mind about the stereotype, then you can come out of that negative mentality.

This freedom from the cheating mentality, in itself, would transform their lives into a more positive flow of prosperity. When you stop thinking about how you can cheat others, you start to focus on how you can help others grow. Prosperity will come much faster.

The reality is that the more successful you become, the more you can help others.

Success has many definitions such as, "measurable progress in a reasonable time." Then one of the other meanings is, "the ideal pursuit of an idea," or what we typically call, "a good ideal." There are various definitions of success, and each person has their definition of success. They can be successful and also be unhappy. The goal of this book is to focus on success on every level ---- how do you become successful, find happiness, and remain successful. That's the key. If you want to stay successful, you have to be in alignment with your true nature which is goodness.

"People Are Out to Get Me"

This happens when the person is suspicious of other people. A friend of mine once told me, "If you only have five dollars, five dollars is a lot of money." What he meant by that is if five dollars is all you've got, then that five dollars mean everything to you. That is the total value you recognize for yourself.

When a person does not have a lot of money, and they're low, they don't have a job, or they don't see opportunity automatically, they have a feeling that everyone around them is out to get them. They don't realize that this is the reason for their poverty and misery in the external world. All they see are the limitations that are surrounding them. That's how they think about life. In order for them to be able to understand this concept that if you see limitations, you get a limited perspective, they need to step outside of their current viewpoint.

When a person is poor, they are attracting others who are also at that level. What happens is the people around them are also low on their luck in life.

When the person is indigent, they don't have money for whatever reason. It could be they never had money, or it could be they had money once and then lost it as a result of the recession or some other financial event. Something happened in their past which has created their limited reality and belief that there is not a lot of money. Either never having money, or the loss of money can impact a person's belief. The worst part of this is that they can't see beyond this belief. They truly feel that's just the way it is.

They believe everyone is out to get them, and they feel like people are trying to keep them where they are. Even in a situation when they are not inferior, they still see other poor people surrounding them because those are the people whom they attract. When you surround yourself with other people who are struggling, each of them is fighting for the same dollar. It becomes a challenge to think that there are good people out there or that the world is abundant.

You need to set the mindset that there are good people out there, and there are people who want to show you the path to abundance. You need to be able to go beyond the fear of scarcity. You want to have a belief that you are deserving of abundance and no one is out to get you.

Then you have to actually get out of your negative environment and negative state. The way to do this is to think of how you can help others. All service is what brings you the money. You give service to others. It could be a service to one person, which could be your employer. Once you have authentically created the most value through your service to your employer, you can start to stretch yourself to provide services to others beyond what you are paid for automatically. This is known as an abundant mindset. The more you give, the more prosperity grows.

When you start to provide service above your paycheck, then you become indispensable to your employer. Any lingering belief that people are out to get you will vanish. When you focus on how you're out to help other people rather than concentrate on the fact that someone else is out to get you, the fear of scarcity will disappear.

It's counterintuitive because people think, "Well, once I'm successful, then I will think about abundance." But it happens in the opposite order. You have to believe there is more than plenty in this world. That means that you give, you create value, you are in service to others, and then the success and the money comes. Money is only exchanged for the value of what's provided.

This is the concept that people often mistake. They

think cash just came for whatever reason. Except for inheritance, money doesn't just appear out of nowhere. Even in the case of inheritance, there's still an exchange of value, which was by luck they got it. The person valued the other person, and that's why he gave it to his son or daughter or whoever it was. It is an exchange of value.

It's actually a very simple formula. Create abundance, and you will receive abundance. The more valuable you can be to others, the more money you can make.

"No One Cares for Me"

This is a destructive mistake many immigrants make. They have the belief, "No one cares for me." I get it. I used to think this too. Several years ago, when I first came to the United States as an immigrant, I was full of negative thoughts. I had the same feeling that everyone was out to get me, and I thought no one would help me.

A mentor and a friend of mine told me, "Why do

you feel this way?" Then I said to him that I felt that I had to protect myself. I felt burdened by the rent that I pay, and I felt like I had to protect myself from all these people who try to cheat me. I told him that I feel like I have to defend myself. I have to take care of my bills, my car payments, and all the expenses to survive. Then he told me, "Well, you're not answering the question. Why do you feel no one cares for you?" Then I said, "They don't care for me because I have to do all this work just to survive." Then I got defiant. I didn't want to be convinced, and I walked away from the conversation.

That day was a turning point for me. It got me thinking in a different way where I was able to reflect and think about what he said. I realized that my thinking was distorted from the struggle I was going through. The belief that no one cares for me turns out that wasn't true at all.

The employer that I worked for did care for me; that's why he gave me a job. Then one day he even called me and said, "Hey Vijai, today is Friday, and you forgot to take your paycheck." Then I said, "I'll take it on Monday." He was saying that he cared for me by reminding me about my paycheck. It was up to me to see it.

I also started to realize that my parents cared for me, and my sister cared for me at that time, my friends cared for me, and my university did care for me as well. Once I opened my eyes to see all the ways they did in fact care for me, it was obvious. That's why they wanted to check up on me time to time to see how I was doing.

This line of thinking that "no one cares for me" is keeping you stuck in a limiting belief. You feel this way because, internally you don't know what to do, or you have a lack of direction on which side you want to proceed, or you don't see success nearby. This happens only when you are in a mindset of deficiency, not abundance. Open your eyes to see all the opportunities around you to let people in. Your heart will open, and you will find that people are kind and generous everywhere when you are open to receive it.

"I Don't Need Others"

This is a very interesting self-limiting belief. It is disguised as making you strong, when in fact it is keeping you stuck.

I've seen many immigrants who come to the United States or anywhere else in the world who also face this limiting belief. The tradition is when they're in their own home or country, they're in the comfort zone. They have many friends. They have many family members who check up on them and who ask them questions, "What are you planning next in your life?" Some of these immigrants would say, "I'm going to study more," or "I'm going to get a job with this company," things of that sort. They have some plans to share, and different family members and neighbors check up on them.

This happens in many countries where they have a strong support system around them. When they come to the US, it's a very individualistic society where you are the only one who measures your progress. Only you can support yourself in achieving your goals. In other words, you don't have anybody checking up on you to see how you're doing.

Some people get cell phone calls from their foreign land when they are living in another country. They might receive calls, and then find out about their parents or friends, but that's just a cell phone call across a phone line. It's different when no one is right in front of you, asking you how you are doing. You start to internalize your feelings, and you start to convince yourself that you don't really need anyone's support.

This is a self-protection measure. You feel it internally that you're doing okay, and you're going to do it your way. You convince yourself you do not have to conform to anybody else's plan because the United States is the land of the free. You don't have to answer to anybody, including your parents or friends or anyone else, not even your elders because you are free. You're going to do it on your terms, and one day you're going to be successful, but you don't know how that success looks like.

You tell yourself, "I'm a unique person." Yes, you are unique, but the only thing is that you still have to stick by your values. You still have to measure your progress, and if you don't do it, you will be uniquely a failure.

It takes an entire cultural shift of thinking like an American. While a lot of the world can perceive Americans as selfish, we have the drive to fulfill our destiny. You can see this American perspective as, "The more I contribute to myself, the better I will be able to serve my family back home."

This uniqueness, according to me, is just a mask that you show to yourself to hide away from the failure that you are not achieving the level of success you want yet. That mask of being unique is your protection. That's what you do. That's what we all do when we are insecure. You tell yourself, "I'm free, and I'm unique. I'm going to do it my way because I'm not making the progress I want to make." You're not taking the necessary steps that are needed to move from point A to point B, which is your ultimate vision.

You do not want to face what's in front of you, and there's no one to ask you except yourself. You may realize that you are accountable to yourself. You are unique. You can make swift progress and then be an instrument of service to your family and hopefully the greater good.

It's important you are making that distinction -- being unique to serve yourself and the greater good is a positive ideal. If you are using the excuse of, "I'm unique, and therefore I can't succeed where I don't fit in," or "this won't work for me," then you're using that defensive thinking as a mask or excuse.

It's a powerful difference to understand which one you are.

Postponing Talent

Several years ago, when I was working for one of my previous employers, I was very innovative, which I still am today. I had brought in several ideas onto the table to this former employer of mine. He would listen to it, and not apply even one of those ideas. As time went by, I decided that "Hey, this employer doesn't realize my value, and I'm not going to give him any more ideas. I'm going to use those ideas for myself when the time is right."

It took me almost ten years before I registered my own company. When I did that, being an implementer, I used all those ideas I had been saving. I started implementing all of those ideas in the first week. The most bizarre thing happened, which was nothing. All those ideas were worthless!

I was holding on to those ideas for ten years, which is a waste of energy, and I postponed my talent for ten years, which made me less talented. For all I knew, if I had seen the ideas for what they were worth, rather than believing in them blindly, I would have had a lot more success much faster. Instead, I chose to limit my capability because I wasn't looking at the reasons why or even asking the former employer, "Why did you not take these ideas into action? What's wrong with them?" I didn't ask him because I was so arrogant and egotistic. I convinced myself that my thoughts were worth millions.

Postponing talent is what many of us do early on in our career, thinking that there's going to be a right time when I'm going to shine and grow and then show the entire universe or world how great I am. However, the problem is, it starts now. You have to shine today. You have to shine now. Start shining now so you can keep shining brighter every day after day.

If you work on that, bringing your talents and the gifts which are given to you by the great Lord, if you're able to do that now, it only builds. You can become brighter and brighter as you go along rather than postponing it. Because if you delay it, you were hiding your shine for several years, and then you want to flash your brilliance all at once. It's going to be a slower process because the start of the shining begins today. It's a compound effect.

Many people think that, if they share their ideas someone is going to steal them, but the most successful people know that the ideas that come through them are meant to be shared. That's back to the abundance mindset, and the abundance thinking is that the more you share your ideas, the better ideas you get. The designs get better and better the more you share them.

You become more skilled at formulating your ideas and sharing them. Your brain would realize this is an idea manufacturing company, and you will manufacture more of those ideas. I love that, the idea manufacturing company. The more you manufacture ideas and share them, the better your ideas become.

The analogy of building muscles can also work here. It's like saying, "I'm not going to use my muscles until it's worth it, or it's imperative, or when I get a chance to show everybody how strong I am." If this is your mentality, then when you do get that opportunity, your muscles aren't going to be strong. They're going to be weak because you haven't been using your muscles. It's the same thing with your ideas. If you think, "I'm going to wait to share my thoughts until I get an opportunity to share those ideas," you are not going to have brilliant ideas to share. If you haven't been sharing them, then you'll have weak idea muscles.

Irritation Towards Others

This self-limiting belief is very interesting. This concept works for any immigrant, not just in the technology sectors; it even works in non-technology industries. It works with immigrants all over the world, not just the United States.

When a person immigrates to a new country, naturally what happens is they look for something different. They've been living a certain way, and they want their life to be changed. They have friends, they have family members, they look a certain way, but they want something different. In that process, they don't know what they want as their highest priority. They didn't go to the country with a clear-cut idea of what they want. They went there without really knowing what they want, and then it's an experiment to figure it out.

In that process, when they see someone from their own home country, what happens is they look at them as competition to what they're doing, and this irritates them. The irritation starts from the simplest of interactions. For example, if the other person who's been in that country for several years comes up and asks them this question, "Where are you from?", the person does not want to answer where they're from because they think that they are not entitled. I mean, this person is not allowed to know where they are from. It's none of his business or her business. They're asking too much. This is a foreign land, and this is not the home country where anybody can speak to anyone. They make up all these rules about how immigrants are supposed to act with one another.

To give an example, when I was with one of my brother-in-law's in London, we went to this Indian store. The person asked my brother-in-law where he was from. He answered, "I'm originally from India." He was living in

London for about a year, and when this person asked him where he was from, he answered, "I'm from India," with a lot of disdain and disrespect on his face. Then, the man who worked at the Indian store turns to me asks me where I'm from. I told him, "I live in Washington DC, and I'm originally from India." I started talking to him, giving him all the information that he was asking for. We had a full conversation. Then, I started asking him questions, and he answered all of the questions. At the end of our pleasant conversation, I asked him for a discount, which he gave me graciously.

We walked out of the Indian store, and then I asked my brother-in-law, "Why are you so angry?" My brother-in-law said, "That was none of his business. If I had come here one year ago or 10 years ago, what does it matter to him? He wants to know too much about me." Then I tell him that could be, but maybe that's not the case. Perhaps he's just making conversation. I gave him all the information, so what if he knows something about me, so what? Maybe you get a new friend.

This attitude of being open did not come naturally to me. It is one that I had to change. I used to be like my brother-in-law when I originally came to the United States.

I didn't want to share information because I thought no one should know what I was doing. That's the mentality of someone who is not destined to be successful. If no one knows what you're doing, you're doing nothing that they could help you with. That's why they don't know what they're doing.

On the other hand, if you have a mentality that you let everyone know what you're doing, and you will share with them everything you're doing, you're coming from a place of strength. Plus, you're also getting their support. Maybe not everyone, but a majority, or even a few people at least would support you with your ideas. You would attract people who support your thoughts, and that way, you at least going to grow with external support.

If you are with the mentality that no one should know what you're doing, no one will ever know. I learned this concept in a very subtle way. I was with the same mentality of, "Why should anyone know what I'm doing? I'm going to become successful, and no one will ever find out about it." I was living with that limiting belief for a few years. One day, when I went to buy my first property, I realized that my employer had to find out about it because he had to confirm to the mortgage broker how much money

I was making. I had to share that information with my employer because the mortgage company was going to call him, which killed me internally. I was obsessing about how he was going to know that I was buying the house.

Then, I had to share my financial information to the banker, and the banker knew how much I was making. It was a full disclosure process to get a house. Everyone in the world knew, and then they put it on the internet that I own that house. I realized afterwards; it's a pretty normal thing that everyone will know if you become successful. You might as well share everything with everyone.

If you're putting walls around you to protect yourself, you believe those walls are working. What you're really doing is you're keeping out the flow of success. The greatest strength is to be vulnerable. That's why when we look at people who can be open, be honest, be authentic and be exposed, we see them as leaders because that's the greatest strength. To be able to lower the walls and lower those protective barriers is the highest level of power. When you have the inner strength, there's no need for protection.

You've created walls that you built which is

senseless because you spend all the energy building those walls, and then those walls are keeping you stuck inside them. It is keeping you unhappy, even if you become successful. Being unhappy and successful in many ways is lonelier than being unsuccessful. You become locked in a prison of your success with no way out.

3Throughout my career, success has always been very important to me. Of course, the definition has changed over the years. The goals have changed as I have gained further experience.

The concept of being happy and prosperous all at the same time is not known to many entrepreneurs or even many people. They think that if they're successful, they're automatically fulfilled. They believe that when they have a car, a house, and then they have kids playing around, they're content. The truth of the matter is, they can have all of the external things that show success on the outside, but they can still feel a void inside of themselves.

This happens all the time. Many people live life to show others they're successful. They want to prove to someone else how successful they are, and they don't live by their own values or their truths. They are not doing the things they really want to do. They are doing it for someone else. Indeed, they have projected success outwards, and they are depressed inside.

An example of this comes from my own life where early on I wanted to get six-pack abs. I took a book, and I read in the book all the steps necessary to get the six-pack abs. The six-pack was essential to me, and I achieved that goal in three months in the year 2013. It took several hours of working out every day and starvation to get to my goal. I was so focused on achieving that six-pack goal; I was not performing at my job well. I was not taking care of my family. Yes, I got my goal. I did get the six-pack abs, and I weighed about 145 pounds with no energy. I looked like a skeleton or a drug addict. I probably wasn't too attractive to look at, and I was unhappy when I got reached my goal. That's when I realized that there is so much more than just achieving your goal.

I realized, "Now that I've got this, so what? I have the picture of me with six-pack abs, so what?" The goal didn't end up fulfilling me like I thought it would. In fact, I felt even more empty than when I started. I felt like a failure despite achieving the success that was important to me, and that made me very unhappy.

An essential thing about success and happiness is how you set up your vision of that goal. You have to realize once you achieve it, what type of impact is it going to create in your life? Will you be happy with that goal? If you ask the right question, you can avoid a lot of pain, energy, and time. Will you be satisfied if you achieve your goal?

If the answer is no, then maybe you have to change the goal, or you have to change your approach towards that goal. What I mean by that is, achieving that six-pack abs in three months of starvation made me unhappy. Later on, I achieved the same six-pack abs by proper nourishment, a proper workout schedule, and with the help from my trainer. I focused my time management while also making sure everybody was happy. I did an excellent job on my job. I was able to contribute my greatest talents at the highest level.

The first approach made me unhappy because the goal was necessary, but I didn't think about the consequences of achieving that goal. I didn't know how I was going to feel once I achieve it. The second time around, I made the same goal, but I knew exactly how I wanted to feel while I was achieving it. I stayed solid in my integrity to my commitments to myself and others. I was very healthy, and also in the process, I was able to contribute to others. That made all the difference. When I achieved the six-pack goal the second time, I was happy. It was the same goal with different results. Today, I am still fit, healthy, and happy keeping the process sustainable.

Chapter 8: Switch Off Your Clock

By this time, you know enough to stop the waiting game. Take the step to plant the seed. Believe that if you do it, you will get the results. If you plant a seed, it is going to take time to germinate. You have to stay focused on it because the universe is going to test you. This is the land of the free, the home of the brave. If you shake quickly and easily, then you're not meant to be here. This isn't the right place for you then. But if you stay committed and you plant the seed, and you trust the tree is going to grow, it will.

It is important for you to realize that as an immigrant, you would do yourself a big favor by surrounding yourself with other people who believe in your dream. This is how you will set up your own community which is made up of people who are committed to the goal of becoming a successful immigrant. These are the ambitious people. Why is it so important for you to find a community of other people that believe in you, will support you and follow you as the trusted advisor? Well, there are some basic facts that will justify that.

You know that as soon as a new law is implemented by the United States Citizenship and Immigration Services, it immediately causes a lot of panic in the immigrant community. People start to wonder what effects it will have on their lives and their careers. Now, some of those laws always existed. The USCIS, which is the United States Citizenship and Immigration Services, keeps amending certain terms in the law. They have a right to go back to the original law. So, immigrants think that this is a new law, but the fact is that it has always existed; it is just amended or reinstated in most cases.

The moment this occurs, what most immigrants do is they start Googling. They put words in Google and search to see how they are going to be impacted, or if there's any information out there for them. Then they start reading forums, which give information about how a certain life changed because of the new law. They read that this person was not able to enter the country again after they were going for a short trip or how they were left jobless and then they had to leave the country because of the change in the law. Reading these forums will give information on only the things that never work for anyone. It will only give rise to more panic. There is a clear need for someone to provide clear-cut information so that people know what they are dealing with.

Make sure to always have trusted advisors who have the right information. This could be attorneys. There's an old saying, "For the right information, you have to pay for it." That's where most people make a mistake. They want the information, but they don't want to pay for it. And they think free information they will get from these forums is going to suffice when it actually will not because it is insufficient and often misleading as well. The forums have negative connotations associated with them anyway.

My father confided that if he had known the secret of a particular process, he could have saved 10 years in his career. It took me several years to realize this. I listened to my father repeating the same thing for many years in many instances. But he never could realize that to know the secret; you have to pay for it. You have to pay in the form of money or in the form of labor you provide to the market place.

I wrote this book for the purpose of giving immigrants the information that they need. This is how I am giving back because I don't want others to go through the same hit-and-miss kind of a situation that I did when I first came to the United States. It helps to learn from another person's experience. It is crucial for all immigrants, prospective as well as existing ones, to know the new immigration secrets from a trusted advisor. I have spent over two million dollars on acquiring all this knowledge and legal advice. I have tested, and I have failed, and that's how I figured everything out. I am offering these secrets to others, so they know not to make the same mistakes.

The book is for the people who want to make it Big in America. There are so many of us who couldn't stand this test of time simply because they didn't know all that was happening, and no one gave them a helping hand. They went back to their own country, not because that's what they originally wanted, but because of their lack of planning, lack of grit, lack of understanding, lack of learning and the strength to face obstacles as they approached them and most importantly lack of support. Are they any better off living in their country of origin? No, my take is that they will face the same thing in their own country unless they have no ambition or vision in the United States.

Then there are some people who have made the conscious decision: "I am going to gain the knowledge and then go back to my country and then serve my people." But that's their clear vision and clear purpose. If that is not your original clear vision and clear purpose and you are trying to compromise, then you are trying to lie to yourself. You start lying to yourself when you are thrown off track, and this will continue in the future. The only way you can stop lying to yourself is by arming yourself with the truth.

If I help people to gain clarity and insight into these rather murky waters of being an immigrant in the United States, I would be very happy. If they approach me and tell me I have helped them in one way or another, I will ask them a question, "What's your goal? How are you going to serve the United States of America?" And if I hear an answer which says they are really going to make a difference to the people in the U.S., immigrants or nonimmigrants, I will feel extremely contented with my life. I will consider it a job well-done.

My goal, my ultimate vision, has been finding ways to serve one billion people on this earth. One billion people may look like a lot if you look at it all together; however, the beauty of that is, if you look at it separately, it will start to make to it seem doable to you. For example, India has 1.5 billion, China is even bigger than that. The United States is about 327 million. The way I see it, if I take three to four countries, and then I serve them, it will take me closer to my goal. In this way, I will serve a billion people in time. Now the other beautiful way to look at this is if I serve one person who has served a billion people, or continues to serve them, then I can still feel like I have achieved my goal. By helping someone who can serve a billion people, I can win. I understand it is just not about me, it is about serving the people.

If I had a book like this when I first came to the United States, I would not have faced the disappointment of watching people behaving differently toward me only because I was an immigrant who came from a different culture. I would have understood that there are cultural differences and I would have known the ways to adjust to them and to make the most of all I had without taking things personally.

My objective with this book is to provide new immigrants as well as the old one with a different perspective. Sometimes, we need someone else to tell us their story, so we can understand our own. That's what I am doing with this book, aside from providing practical guidelines. If this book helps just one person, I would feel like the universe has just started the spark, which can ignite the entire world leading to a fire of prosperity.

My hope is that you take the spark that lives inside of you and you share it with the world. The Statue of Liberty represents this spark of prosperity that all individuals have a right to life, liberty, and justice.

Summary

People have asked me, "Why are you giving this much information away in this book?" I am sharing all of this with you because I believe in my core that knowledge is infinite. The beauty of evolution is that when you grow, you are able to give to others on a greater level. When you give your knowledge, your awareness increases. When you teach, you learn. When you share, you receive. It's an endless cycle of abundance that's going to make you wiser, stronger, and better at who you are at your core essence. By sharing openly and freely, you are continuing to move towards that which is infinite.

In many ways, this book is a symbol of what I am demonstrating with my life. I am explaining what I am teaching. I am living what I am preaching.

This is the greatest honor of my life. You can live your life and be a role model, and also create other role models. That's how you can create a society that's truly aligned with the highest levels of abundance. That's the dream that I have. I hope you will share it with me and the others who are impacted by this philosophy that is shared in this book.

My desire for you is that you keep taking action. My hope is that you keep growing because it never ends.

My greatest wish is that you always stay open and believe in your dreams. People need some belief system that they can see exists because they know truly inside that they are good people. You know truly inside those big dreams of yours can be achieved.

Many people don't find something to use as a reference for them to believe that their dreams are possible. Though they understand the belief at their core, it is a shock because of the external conditions which can kill their dreams. When you align with other successful people, you can model what they have done, and then become successful quickly while making a difference in the universe.

The United States of America is the perfect partner for this unlimited, infinite creation of your dreams into reality. It's the number one country because it has everything. The fairness, the integrity, the kindness, the strength, the power, the bravery, everything is instilled in one country. It's really a mirror because whatever you put out is going to be reflected back to you.

Everything that you're getting in this book is the key to becoming a successful immigrant and ultimately a contributor to the United States and the world. This is so important to me when you read this book that you continue to flourish and grow. You can contribute to the greater good by supporting the United States of America and providing all this great country has to offer to the rest of the world.